Shaun,
Happy Xmas 2005
Love
    Sister, Maeve X

DITCHDIGGERS
AND
FAIRYTHORNS

GUILDHALL PRESS

PAT COWLEY

DITCHDIGGERS
AND
FAIRYTHORNS

Poems by Michael Healy
Paintings by Pat Cowley

For Hannah and Christine

First published in November 2005

Guildhall Press
Unit 15
Ráth Mór Business Park
Bligh's Lane
Derry BT48 0LZ
T: (028) 7136 4413 F: (028) 7137 2949
info@ghpress.com www.ghpress.com

Foreword

The Poet and the Painter
Homer's ghost came whispering to my mind.
He said: I made the Iliad from such
A local row. Gods make their own importance.

Epic by Patrick Kavanagh

There is a seam running through much Irish poetry that is rooted in a sense of place. Think of Kavanagh's Monaghan or Heaney's Derry; poetry that both records and transcends the local, the commonplace, the feel and smell and sound of the poet's known world. As Kavanagh says, the Iliad started with a local row.

Most of Michael Healy's poems inhabit and in some ways reclaim Donegal. There are poems set elsewhere, of course, in Derry, on Glenshane Pass, in Mullaghmore but the locus of the collection is Donegal. It is not, however, the Donegal of increasing industrialisation; nor is it the county of holiday homes and haciendas, *'a world that no longer/Sees nor cares/How water gets away.'* The work is more elemental in its concerns; *Stones, Draining, Fencing, A Rutted Field, Hedges, Samhain;* the very titles suggest a poet whose antennae are tuned to the natural world around him, a world in which there are walls to repair, fences to put in place, cattle to be foddered, the recurring rituals of rural existence on the north-western seaboard. But the poems are not simply a matter of record; they are probings, excavations, the poet's way of getting to the essence of things. This is poetry that digs beneath the topsoil.

Echoes of history are threaded through the work, soundings of the past, both distant and recent. This is a Donegal where a visit to *Grianan Well* can trouble *'the ripples/Of what happened here'* and draw down again, *'The rattle/Of spears upon/*

Their ancient shields.' In *Boat Trip,* the poem remembers an act of violence that has marked forever the landscape in which it happened.

But this is not just a collection of poetry. Pat Cowley's paintings find their visual inspiration in much the same geographical territory that shapes Michael Healy's poems. I am fortunate to have two of his works here in London, one of Derry seen from the Waterside at daybreak on the new millennium and another of Horn Head, County Donegal. Yet the paintings in the book are not direct reflections on the poems, nor are the poems deliberate interpretations of the paintings. This is a collaboration, a coming together, based on shared sensibilities, of poetry and painting that has at its core an affinity with the place in which both men set their work. As with the best such collaborations, the poems and the paintings illuminate each other; they force us to look closely and read carefully. The resonances are well worth the effort.

Michael Healy and I were school friends. I have a very clear memory of the two of us heading off one summer into Donegal to watch a solar eclipse. We made our way to Grianan Fort and stood on the battlements until low cloud and late afternoon rain defeated us. There was a sense nonetheless of the elemental all around us, of the Earth and the Heavens at their perennial work. That sense has carried on into these poems. I hope you enjoy reading them in the company of Pat Cowley's fine paintings.

Gary McKeone
London, October 2005

Biographies

The Poet

Michael Healy's love of the land and the people who inhabit it is firmly rooted in his family history in farming, fostered by his late father Frank.

A former pupil of St Columb's College in Derry, he graduated in medicine from Queen's University Belfast in 1984 and holds a masters degree in medical law from the University of Wales, Cardiff, 2003. He is currently a full-time general practitioner in the Waterside area of Derry.

This book is his first venture into print and includes poems from his Charles Macklin Autumn School award-winning collection.

The Painter

Pat Cowley lives and works in Derry. Educated at the Belfast College of Art and the University of Ulster, he was head of art at Saint Peter's High School in Derry. But as demand grew for his work, Pat moved on to concentrate on his career as a professional artist.

His work has been exhibited extensively in Ireland and further afield in London, New York and Boston.

Much of Pat's inspiration comes from the same Donegal landscape of hills, shores and derelict farmhouses as Michael Healy's poetry and he has previously illustrated several successful books including *City of Derry* and *Donegal Highlands*.

Contents

Snáthadán

A word that danced
In the air, delicate,
So close to loss
We reached out
To cradle it,
Minds and tongues
To caress,
A thread finely woven
Through a poem
Knitted in our bones.
From the chrysalis
A daddy long legs
Was born.

Glentogher

I would come down off the hill,
A Shogun warrior descending
Upon the fold,
A modern Cynddylan unseeing,
Through legend and dreams,
Of elfin silver and gold,
Sapphires, emeralds and rubies,
Scouring their way
Roadside with the river,
On to Carn.
I remember your small hands
That brought me treasures
Trawled with a discerning eye,
Excitement in a pebble,
Perfect rounded pleasure
In "A good one?"
And the riches it might buy.
What unfathomed prizes lay
Within that ancient tract,
Might lie there even yet,
Had there been pause
To pan the stream?
But I chased fool's gold,
The river rolled on
With no turning back,
And childhood lost its gleam.

Looking for gold

Children of the Ebb Tide

Compulsion drove us here,
You off wind and tide unbridled,
Passed riding hulks at anchor
Through heaving Atlantic weather.
I from a warmer berth
Broached the twitching farmyard gate
To feel the tethered force
Of pulsing muscle quick deceived
By lure of fur and feather.
Whilst others aground lonelier broughs
Relieved of dreamstreams' cloistered pools
Raw feel that ebbing flow,
Destinies enmeshed, subdued,
Tarnished silver under priestly blows.

Shelter from the storm

The Fixer

"Made for it!"
He'd joyfully proclaim,
Sympathy for the rejected stone
Pleasure in making whole,
The triumph of discarded scrap
Even better employed
In another role.
The final sugh
His trademark touch
A turn too much,
That stripped the thread,
Broke the handle
And cracked the pane,
Creative make-does
That still remain,
Stood the test
While he is dead.

The Fixer

A Rutted Field

Black land never meant
To carry more when wet
Than sheep or snipe,
And yet,
The figure eight
Weeping dent
Of tractor trailer
Fully loaded,
Turned and twisted
Till green exploded.
Ground rented,
For that
Not respected,
Two tracks
Two wills
Collided.

A Dead Calf and a Stranger

Between the two
Neither could say
Why one had lived,
The other not.
"Keep beasts,
Expect losses"
The wisdom
That pulled them
Through.
While in the corner field,
Downwind riffling the clover,
Life's breath jolted the survivor,
They extolled
The dusted carcass,
And struggled,
That this
Should bring them closer.

A Rushy Field

Decades of lime
Toil and till,
Counting now
For nil.
After his time
A cancer seed
That slept
And bided,
As if it heard
Last prayers recited,
Broke cover
In the clover,
Knowing
He could not
Slash and burn,
Dig a drain
Or turn a furrow.
Under limpet
Rosaries of rush,
Slow burning
Creep and crush,
Emerald envy faded
And surrendered too.

A rushy field

Draining

Only for every third step
The hoarse stone
Against complaining steel,
Somewhere between snipe and corncrake.
Only for the prying eye,
A placed bicycle and raincoat,
Offered to the sky
The biscuit tin for your viaticum.
You might not even be there,
Might as well not be,
For a world that no longer
Sees nor cares
How water gets away.

Glengad (The Farm not Bought)

No purpose could be found
In your purchase on this ground.
A more nimble thief
Stepped your march
On this hill of thieves
To suck the breath
More than gradient allowed.
A bargain struck
In fragile words
But a deal not done.
"Once I waited for you, my son,
Now you must wait for me."

Bailer-binder

Scuttled and simmering
In mid-summer's whine,
Threaded now with spider web
Not binder twine,
A frozen bailer reef
Awash the meadowsweet
Memory only saved,
Fossil reminder
Of an ancient rural grief.
A boy's blue geansaí
Repeatedly dismembering,
Knitting,
Through the golden hay.

Haymaking

The Rush

Sucked to the wet
You'd think
Its name
Belied that stance.
And yet,
On black land
Acid rotten,
Rain sodden,
A season's lapse
Only half a chance,
Sends sleeping seeds
To peep and probe
Where beasts have trodden.
In that moment
Your back is turned,
The green erodes
And fields get stolen.

Stones

Any stone could make a wall,
With one more turn to make it fit
One more squint to remember it.
Shown lesser care upon the reject cairn
Of malformed flint with keep to earn,
Made fill a hole,
To lose its soul,
Being trodden on.

The Country Buffoon

Only a moment
It must have been,
Your eye caught mine
And let me in,
To see the weight
Of cruel chance
And grinding lot,
That left your place now
To play the fool
For strangers' company.
Then I ashamed
Of my part in the pack,
Turned my back
To slink away.
Yet to this day,
You now in Earth's embrace,
I have not forgotten
That look upon your face.

Bartalk

Hitch-hiker

The rhythm of home
Was in us both
Though mine beat
Two hundred miles
To the wrapped hum
Of the Vauxhall.
Hypnotised by the
Splintered light
I could not stop
Despite your stare
And found a thousand
Reasons why
I'd been right
To leave you

Standing there,
Rain splattered
And tattle haired,
Though further on
I could not, still
Cannot say
If it was your face,
That look, or,
Just your presence
In that lonely place,
I know I was wrong
To drive away,
And wonder still
If you got home.

Haymaker

"Make hay
While the sun shines,"
So they say, and
Being made in public
When one mistake
Could lose the golden prize,
Best heed the wise
Well meant advice.
But come the day
The weather fines
Though yet a little bruckle,
It's now your choice
Or not to make
Under not just
One discerning eye,
Begin the struggle
The anxious race,
Save the hay
Or lose your face.

School Friends

Your hand outstretched
Across twenty years
Although your face
Etched quizzical with doubt
Questioned who or what
This unexpected greeting was about.
And I, having started it,
To end the game
Watched focus dawning
Frame by frame,
On the offer of my name.

School friends

Awesome

A half time
Throw in
To a game
We could,
Should, still win.
Untethered,
You were awesome.
Doubt sidelined
Outside the square
With those grown line bound,
Your knowing grin
Didn't care
From whom
Or where
The gift had come.

One of Us

On your knees
You watch this man
White surplice
On black soutane,
Such a shining
Holy face
Our father
Who art
Full of grace.
Bread aloft
Transfigured he stands
And so you see
The nicotine
On his hands.

Fencing

Clubbed under iron
Tanalised years melted.
Black ground sucked, as if,
To pull tree from sledge
Would cheat the child's
Mizzled embrace.
Forty years, you and I,
A job put off; fencing.
Yours now to grasp
And mine to cast,
The careless glance
That bruised the edge.

Mending fences

The Bitter Word

Yellowed and vulpine,
Twisted and disappointing
As the road
That should rise up
To meet you
But deceitfully runs away.
Through pats of smoke
That semaphored
The bottom of
Too many mornings,
Too many let downs
And little expectation,
His lip curled
To savour,
Not like a man
Black pint in hand,

But the cur
In the street,
That bit first
Then licked
Salt off his wounds,
And shite off
A thistle,
Detested himself,
Detested his neighbour,
And though it never
Tasted that good,
Through bile
And spittle,
Couldn't resist
To retaliate first
With the bitter word.

Repaired

Xylophone spar on a kitchen floor
Announced your presence there,
Pencilled memory in a broken chair,
Reluctant repair fragile once more.
Black graphite wood teacher precise,
Tight grain chosen with care,
Holding you now under our prayer,
No sign then of the oak's clamp-like vice.
The wood sounded, soft spoke-
Whispers through the divining rod,
Of cartwheels furrowing the covering sod,
Of grains of senses sleeping in ground unbroke.

Draining

No modern panacea could provide
That comfort in your hide,
Fastened by the suck of muck
Ambition drowned in an endless shough.
Rhythmic rasp of stone on steel
So hypnotised you could not feel
The careless arc and careful edge.
With freedom now to disengage
Crimson sparkled cold on black
Hurried away with no look back.
A simple accident on a wee hill farm
Or lonely act of deliberate self harm?

Wee hill farm. Urris

Halting Site

Somewhere between
Ballyshannon and Ballysadare
A gently sloping lay-by,
European conquest survivor,
Embraced me,
Tired beyond care;
An overhead gantry
Simplicity by design
Terrible in execution
Discrimination stitch welded
To concentrated perfection,
Its chevroned waspish warning
No height restriction
More race and colour bar,
Proclaimed that other travellers
Were not so welcome,
Though generations' instincts
Yearly drew them there.
Somewhere between
Stalingrad and Sligo
Another time,
Another world ago,
A million feet ill shod
Trod their own
Dreary highways,
Followed every instruction,
Passed intolerance shrines,
Apparently unseeing,
Hatreds once hidden in
The ordinariness of construction.

Derelict Waterwheel

A three-sixty promise
Of three-sixty-five
Circadian rhythms
Arced to binary,
Fluid rotations abandoned.
Yesterday's labours
Memory only now,
Scutched coiled codes
Milling our circulation.

Mick, Pat, Joe, Dan

The frosted indignance
Of unfoddered beasts
Could not halt now
His call to the bar.
Beneath the silage scented
Fog of rustic wit
And counter spin,
Of the herd
Yet so alone,
Within
His blackout skin.

Foddering

Mermaid

Let down your hair
To tumble on the rocks below,
Smash in crystals
That sparkle once
Then disappear.
Surrender to the sú
Of sand and drift,
Uaigneas,
You care not
To lift,
There's no-one there
To see or care
Let down your hair.

Northerly gale. Isle of Doagh

Grianan Well

It was high summer
Too many summers ago,
When you and I,
Giddy on holiday,
Cycled out from Derry,
Passed Bertie
And his cones,
Through Bridgend
For the long push,
Upwards, to the fort
At Grianan.

Something seemed lost
There, in the rebuilding.
As if the Ui Neill
No longer slumbered
Their watch,
Eternally doomed,
To lie fitful

Beneath skylarks
Marking time,
Bobbing the hill.

Yet at the well,
Your hands
Could not resist
The cool mist-
Moist invitation,
Fisting through
The cleansings
For wishful pennies,
To the mossy
Fronds within.

As if you'd delved
Too deep,
And touched a nerve,
Troubled the ripples,

Of what happened here,
The hill powered down
And held its breath,
Finger tight to lip.
Then exhaled
From nowhere
A thunderous brattle,
The rattle
Of spears upon
Their ancient shields.

You'd remember now
If I had you here,
Her sullen
Baleful stare,
Her breath,
Hot,
Upon our necks.

The holy well. Grianan

Mull

We had stood
In an eagle's fix,
By a frozen tarn,
Gripped in the rim
Like a frosted lens
Awaiting the polisher's
Skilful kiss.
A Scotch pine,
Weary of the struggle
Had given up,
Its impetiginous root,
A scab of earth
Skywards in salute.

I thought of it now
Twenty years further on,

Disgorged at Cairnryan
And heading northwards
Once again,
Through the permafrost
Of memory;

Wondered if the
Wound had healed,
Or did the ground still wait
The tree's return
Of all it held
Within its grip,
Letting slip, the
Glittering shards
Of recollection,
Tangled in my mind?

On Christmas Eve

The chapel air is sharp-spiked
With crack of pew,
Rustle and whisper
Of children,
Trying to be reverent.
Old woman's prayerful whistling
Tumbles the aisle
Eroding the mind's paralysis.

Hawthorns (for Finbar)

It was hawthorn, he told me,
To set me thinking,
That he'd missed the most,
Exiled in a land of lilac.
A gentle bush on its own,
No spike or thorn
To ward or warn,
Where unseen sprites
Might gather under
Sparkling moonlight skies,
To practice ancient elfin rites
Away from prying eyes.
And no-one wise
Would ever dare

To cut a stick from there
That at the hireling fair
In temper quick, could feel
The flesh and splinter bone.
Though tamed in rows
Marks different leys
And different ways
In blizzard white that fades,
To the burning bush
Of winter, where the scholar,
Fingers pressed to book and lip
Darts like the skiting
Blackbird with his ringled eye,
Amongst the tangle of our roots.

The fairy bush

Cancer Collusion

A yellow streak
On starched white,
I could not hold
Your marbled grin
Painted eager
By the grip within.
As if now to please
Could somehow
Twist your odds,
We both conspire
To ignore
These runes
Much read before.

Sleep

The boy slept, shucked
In the voices of women,
An ebb tide of fever
Sucked the curtain,
Shivered in sheets
Green and vernal
Like marram on the dune.

They took comfort
In the clatter of busy tea-cups
And the low rumble
Of a Hoover
Furrowing carpet below.
In awestruck whispers
Skirting how close
They'd come,
To loss.

Malin Bridge

Two centuries'
Tidal ebb and flow.
Silently observed
Comings and goings.
The nine-eyed bridge
Would know
What passes under
Has always come back
What crosses over
Not always so.

Evening. Malin

Conacre

Knowing what he would find,
October's hip-garnered wisdom
Drove him out,
The foot of the Master
Being worth four of his hands.
November's promised
Trespass reward
No salve or balm
To the aching track
Of a stranger's touch,
For poached lands
And a gate unbarred.

Shooting

Two men, two dogs
Four together
No worries, no fuss.
One purpose,
Focus on the sloping
Jinking break
For the freedom
Of another
Night of fear,
That ended in the searing
Crash to Earth,
Who mothered all of us.

Boat Trip

A simple pleasure
For royal blood
That ruled the seven seas,
All the way from Burma,
It ended here.
Sluicing shards
Of cold green spray
In the after silence
Barely lapped
Upon the quay.
Amidst the lager
Ice cream
And kiss me quick,
The chafing ropes
Of memory
Bind them to this shore.
The wee pier shudders
Still struggles,
To wash the stain away;
It could even be today.
And will be
For evermore.

Boat trip

Snow on Glenshane

A duvet fell flake to flake,
Smothering the tail-light snake,
Of tarmacadam umbilical
Carrying on every axle,
Missions of love and trade,
Loves lost, deals made,
Violent histories of the feared,
Slumber mysteries of the disappeared,
Promises in safety broken,
On a road not open.
Shut down, severed, cut off,
Gaza of the North,
Where in the bitter cold,
If truth were told,
We do not bemoan, those
Stolen frozen moments on our own.

Just Me

So here I am
Quiet and alone.
Silence!
Except for the clock,
And thoughts
That I own.

The Last Shot

Perhaps a woodcock,
A full moon free faller
From Siberian hardships,
Made his bed,
Pressed the earth,
Drab in dread.
Holding saucer-eyed,
Tight to trust
From his birch
And alder brush;
Surveyed us three,
Draped and misted,
Twisted wraiths of breath
That coughed and fumbled
As December twilight
Folded in and tumbled
About our heads.
Two fields, two shoughs
A barbed wire fence
To tear at tired legs,
And then,
The gradient back.
"Too old, too tired,
Too late, too far."
Only the dog would know
The mistake he scented
As we turned away contented
Towards our beds,
Through the weeping snow.

Snow

Gable

A thousand
North Atlantic storms
Barged up and over
The russet scallop roof,
Until the jellied peat
Upon which it stood,
Quivered and heaved,
Shivered as if, tree-like,
It would soon uproot,
While winnowing fingers,
Sucked the slaked lime
Of a thousand re-kindlings;
And though holding
Yet its ground,
No longer could contain
The heart heat
Long since leached away,
Westwards,
Through the hearthscar
In the stones.

Gable

By the Fort (The Dublin Express)

White pony cropping
Grass red with blood
History's droppings
Leaves his print in the mud.
Silent stones watching
Patient and still
Internally sketching
Memories on a hill.

Carraignabreaghy Castle

Grubbers and Ploughs

Girlish colours that seem to mock
Trundle wheel and moth-eaten sock,
What do they mean now,
The grubber and the plough?
Painted silent, anchored, frozen,
Ornaments on ground unbroken.
Redundant tillers on a lawn
Testimony to times now gone,
Tea-stained sweat that glistered
Hands, cracked and blistered,
Spancelled to the creaking harness
Through midgey dusk to relieving darkness.
Why do we keep them, exalted there?
As if to show we give a care
For furrows, straight wide and deep,
Their length a struggle, a family to keep,
For backs that broke to get us here
To garden unyoked of hunger fear?
Or do we paint them yellow and black,
And hope those times might not come back?

The Cuckoo

May's Angelus peals
Clean and clear,
A pause across the fields,
Butter fat on lean air,
To ponder how
Things were, are now
And could be yet.
She sings her songs and goes,
Siren parasitic promises
Delight another year,
While we strain to hear,
To shed our woes,
Ignore our wrongs,
Too eager to forget
Treachery and regret,
And those who were
Taken from us.

Samhain

Mid-Samhain as Earth tumbled
Deeper into northern darkness,
Autumn forgiveness yielded
To the bitter reproach of winter;
An unchecked planet careering the void,
Solitary solace, a folding invitation
That coiled towards the tide.
He lost himself again beyond reach.

What unseen string
By water's edge
Plucked and pulled,
Sounded in deadened ear?
Wearily he broke away
To hunch against the turn
Of yet another year.

First snow. Sliabh Sneacht

Healy not Heaney

Thirty years now
In an eyrie
Above the schoolyard
Where he held forth
Round and round
The Marble Arch,
Fifty-fifty
Of hoss and rabbit
Was rabbit pie,
One of its legs
Being both the same,
Scorn rained on the man
Who dug with a pen
And not a spade.
My meter beat
To the slip-slap
Of his digging,
Knowing that I too
Could turn a sod
Though the going
Would be harder,
Grow spuds
If not potatoes.

The Blind Fiddler

His fretting fingers
Brailed mountain stories,
Wisps of betrayal,
Moss stained
Smoke ingrained
Flights from revenue,
Hound and redcoat.
Headlong through darkness
I followed him
As best I could,
Crashed mountain ash,
Alder, gorse and hawthorn,
Ran wooded glens
To the glassy lough
Till the flesh was torn.
There as always
Crabbing the shingle,

Splitting the slick
With creaking oars
And conspiratorial voices,
A boat awaits,
Stealing bonny princes
Away to distant shores,
Where gypsy kings
Make bad choices
And broken hearts
Are never mended.
A single tear
Imploded beneath
The rosined bridge,
When the music ended,
It was clear
That he could see
As well as any there.

Viking

Did your longboat slip the sound,
Noiseless on the flow?
Or brazen, full sheets a-blow,
Natives, rabbits put to ground?

Centuries on now,
Where they laid you and how,
Probed in violation, perhaps retaliation,
Digitally displayed, sampled, DNA'ed.

The essence of their quest
Their academic conceit,
That the dead might again learn to speak,
Glars the knowledge that they seek;
Reeks to the stench of the ebb.

On the history channel,
An untrammelled beast

Of rape and pillage,
Proven in field and fjord,
Roams lost, through Valhalla,
Without shield or sword,
Sheathed in a drawer,
Cardboard crated, with bones,
Torn from their warrior.

Will no-one hear your
Rage in the night,
For lost generations
And stolen burial rite?

Eternally caged in mass concrete
I pray you might rise again,
From deep in the foundations,
Raid their global village,
From the halls of the slain!

The mouth of the Foyle

Snipe

The scréach,
A wisp of breath
That palmed the moss,
Pushed watery Earth
Headlong downwind,
Its careering flight
A will-o'-the wisp,
Of ordinary perfection,
Like a word
In ones and noughts,
Bits and bytes
Clattering off
The keyboard,
That could not
Be caught,
Would not be
In the story.
And I bogbound
Stuttered and stumbled,
Fumbled the shot,
Never to see you
Ever again.

Ballycroy

Walkers

A lone beachcaster
Who stood against the tide
Was asked a hundred times
Of luck but never once
His purpose.
What drove them there
From car park to corner river,
The reason for the quest?
Much more than merely
Making room for,
Or catching dinner.

Walkers. Lisfannon

The Turn Away

"God's tears on a rainy funeral,"
Or so they'd have liked to say,
As hand over hand they payed
You in, in delicate balance,
To rest in clabbering clay.
As the last ripples of ritual
Eddied around the stones,
Weepers surged over sleepers
And hand over hand they paid
Clasped handshakes and solemn vows,
Promises never to be kept,
Like grasps of a knotted rope
That hand over hand
Allowed them ebb away.
While on the edge, no-one wept,
I eyed a sodden rook
That breasted the sycamore,
I've seen him there before,
Thought of souls taking flight
Dark companions through the night,
Promised I would keep
The memory that I took,
Then lost the indelicate balance,
Fleeing last handshakes at the gate
For the comforting diminuendo
Of departing.

The Sprayer

As malachite rushes
Shivered in the holm
Too late for them now
His passing,
They stepped the street
As he would the field,
With studied care,
Slow to part
The measure of the man.
Seventy-five turnings,
Comings and goings,
Rolling, spraying,
Breaking and repairing.

The Watcher

Briefly, a curtain net
Swept across the window pane,
Gentle but hurried,
Like a wayward sprung curl
Smoothed and replaced
On a girl's flustered brow,
Gathered in its nictitating wake
A hawk's view, pixel by pixel.
It was the poet's eye though
That dreamt the narrative,
And told the story
Frame by frame,
Be it right or wrong,
It was what she saw,
How she saw it,
What she spoke to herself.

The Watcher

Wake House

Shrouded for the journey,
His coracle rowed
An awkward sea;
A traveller disconnected,
Although it seemed
He'd much to say,
And would've more
On another day.
As to his lee
They built a shed,
Westwards in dispute
A boundary by his head,
Through sympathising throng,
Your eye held mine
A moment, just too long,
To offer simply tea.
"Ah well," they'd say,
"Life must go on."

Passage

Hedges

His hedges were
Always better kept
Than the other
Side of the house,
With sculpted walls
And flat on top,
No rusted wire
Nor posts uncapped,
Or rubbish where
Birds get trapped.
Theirs unruly,
Wayward, untended,
Full of holes,
Trespass intended,

Where gaps unmended,
Are wide spaced eyes
That tell the tale,
Who bent the knee,
Beyond the Pale
At transfiguration.
A country scene,
The land divided,
An unread script
In strangers' hands,
Who wouldn't care,
Could not know
Or understand, that here,
Hedges found religion.

Hedges

Fencing

Even then,
I could see
That post and I
Were seen as one.
Lost in the focus,
Of a job not done
Once more to sweeten it
The hammer swung.

An Focal Searbh

Chroith an duilleog le himeacht an éin,
Mar chroí briste breoite ag bualadh go dian;
Smaoineamh seachránach a cheiliúir san aer,
Le cogar fáinleoige ag eitilt sa spéir,
Cuimilt a heiteog mar lámha cneasta mná.
Anois i m'aonar leis an fhearg ag trá,
Ba mhaith liom greim seabhaic 'fháil air,
An focal sin searbh a bhí ráite aréir.